Thomas Campbell

The Pleasures of Hope

Third Edition

Thomas Campbell

The Pleasures of Hope
Third Edition

ISBN/EAN: 9783337091538

Printed in Europe, USA, Canada, Australia, Japan

Cover: Foto ©Andreas Hilbeck / pixelio.de

More available books at **www.hansebooks.com**

THE PLEASURES OF HOPE.

By THOMAS CAMPBELL.

ILLUSTRATED BY
BIRKET FOSTER, GEORGE THOMAS, AND HARRISON WEIR.

THIRD EDITION.

LONDON:
SAMPSON LOW, SON, AND MARSTON,
MILTON HOUSE, LUDGATE HILL.

LONDON:
R. CLAY, SON, AND TAYLOR, PRINTERS,
BREAD STREET HILL.

ILLUSTRATIONS.

PART I.

		Page
At summer eve, when heaven's aërial bow . . .	BIRKET FOSTER . .	1
The way-worn pilgrim seeks thy summer bower .	BIRKET FOSTER .	3
The wolf's long howl from Oonalaska's shore .	HARRISON WEIR .	4
Pierced the deep woods	BIRKET FOSTER . .	7
When Venus, throned in clouds of rosy hue . .	BIRKET FOSTER .	9
Bright as the pillar rose at Heaven's command .	BIRKET FOSTER . .	11
Her silent watch the mournful mother keeps .	GEORGE THOMAS	12
Or lisps with holy look his ev'ning prayer .	GEORGE THOMAS .	14
Piled on the steep, her blazing faggots burn . .	HARRISON WEIR .	16
Leans o'er its humble gate, and thinks the while	BIRKET FOSTER . .	17
There shall the flocks on thymy pasture stray .	HARRISON WEIR .	19
His trusty warriors, few, but undismay'd . . .	GEORGE THOMAS .	21
Tell's Chapel—Lake of Lucerne	BIRKET FOSTER . .	25
And braved the stormy spirit of the Cape .	BIRKET FOSTER . .	29
Tail-piece—Ship in sight of harbour .	BIRKET FOSTER .	31

PART II.

Who hath not paused, while Beauty's pensive eye .	GEORGE THOMAS	. 33
In vain the wild bird caroll'd on the steep . .	HARRISON WEIR	. 35
And the lone cuckoo sighs along the vale . . .	HARRISON WEIR	. 37
Some pleasing page shall charm the solemn hour	GEORGE THOMAS	. 39
And arms and warriors fell with hollow clang .	HARRISON WEIR	. 41
From Kilda to the green Ierne's shore . .	BIRKET FOSTER .	. 43
Bethlehem's shepherds in the lonely vale .	BIRKET FOSTER .	. 46

ANALYSIS OF PART I.

The Poem opens with a comparison between the beauty of remote objects in a landscape, and those ideal scenes of felicity which the imagination delights to contemplate. — The influence of anticipation upon the other passions is next delineated. An allusion is made to the well-known fiction in Pagan tradition, that, when all the guardian deities of mankind abandoned the world, Hope alone was left behind.—The consolations of this passion in situations of danger and distress.—The seaman on his midnight watch.— The soldier marching into battle.—Allusion to the interesting adventures of Byron.

The inspiration of Hope, as it actuates the efforts of genius, whether in the department of science, or of taste.—Domestic felicity, how intimately connected with views of future happiness.—Picture of a mother watching her infant when asleep.—Pictures of the prisoner, the maniac, and the wanderer.

From the consolations of individual misery, a transition is made to prospects of political improvement in the future state of society.—The wide field that is yet open for the progress of humanizing arts among uncivilised nations.— From these views of amelioration of society, and the extension of liberty and truth over despotic and barbarous countries, by a melancholy contrast of ideas we are led to reflect upon the hard fate of a brave people recently conspicuous in their struggles for independence.—Description of the capture of Warsaw, of the last contest of the oppressors and the oppressed, and the massacre of the Polish patriots at the bridge of Prague.—Apostrophe to the self-interested enemies of human improvement.—The wrongs of Africa.—The barbarous policy of Europeans in India.—Prophecy in the Hindoo mythology of the expected descent of the Deity to redress the miseries of their race, and to take vengeance on the violators of justice and mercy.

THE PLEASURES OF HOPE.

AT summer eve, when heav'n's aërial bow
Spans with bright arch the glittering hills below,
Why to yon mountain turns the musing eye,
Whose sunbright summit mingles with the sky?
Why do those cliffs of shadowy tint appear
More sweet than all the landscape smiling near?--

'Tis distance lends enchantment to the view,
And robes the mountain in its azure hue.

Thus, with delight, we linger to survey
The promis'd joys of life's unmeasur'd way;
Thus, from afar, each dim-discover'd scene
More pleasing seems than all the past hath been;
And every form, that Fancy can repair
From dark oblivion, glows divinely there.

What potent spirit guides the raptur'd eye,
To pierce the shades of dim futurity?
Can Wisdom lend, with all her heav'nly power,
The pledge of Joy's anticipated hour?
Ah, no! she darkly sees the fate of man—
Her dim horizon bounded to a span;
Or, if she hold an image to the view,
'Tis Nature pictur'd too severely true.

With thee, sweet Hope! resides the heav'nly light,
That pours remotest rapture on the sight:
Thine is the charm of life's bewilder'd way,
That calls each slumb'ring passion into play:
Wak'd by thy touch, I see the sister band,
On tiptoe watching, start at thy command,
And fly where'er thy mandate bids them steer
To Pleasure's path, or Glory's bright career.

Primeval Hope, the Aönian Muses say,
When Man and Nature mourn'd their first decay;
When every form of death, and every woe,
Shot from malignant stars to earth below;

When Murder bar'd its arm, and rampant War
Yok'd the red dragons of her iron car;
When Peace and Mercy, banish'd from the plain,
Sprung on the viewless winds to Heav'n again;
All, all forsook the friendless guilty mind,
But Hope, the charmer, linger'd still behind.

Thus, while Elijah's burning wheels prepare,
From Carmel's height, to sweep the fields of air,
The prophet's mantle, ere his flight began,
Dropp'd on the world—a sacred gift to man.

Auspicious Hope! in thy sweet garden grow
Wreaths for each toil, a charm for every woe:
Won by their sweets, in Nature's languid hour,
The way-worn pilgrim seeks thy summer bower;

There, as the wild-bee murmurs on the wing,
What peaceful dreams thy handmaid spirits bring!
What viewless forms th' Æolian organ play,
And sweep the furrow'd lines of anxious thought away!

Angel of life! thy glittering wings explore
Earth's loneliest bounds, and Ocean's wildest shore.
Lo! to the wint'ry winds the pilot yields
His bark careering o'er unfathom'd fields;

Now on Atlantic waves he rides afar,
Where Andes, giant of the western star,

With meteor standard to the winds unfurl'd,
Looks from his throne of clouds o'er half the world.

Now far he sweeps, where scarce a summer smiles,
On Behring's rocks, or Greenland's naked isles;
Cold on his midnight watch the breezes blow,
From wastes that slumber in eternal snow;
And waft, across the waves' tumultuous roar,
The wolf's long howl from Oonalaska's shore.

Poor child of danger, nursling of the storm,
Sad are the woes that wreck thy manly form!
Rocks, waves, and winds the shatter'd bark delay
Thy heart is sad, thy home is far away.

But Hope can here her moonlight vigils keep,
And sing to charm the spirit of the deep:
Swift as yon streamer lights the starry pole,
Her visions warm the watchman's pensive soul:
His native hills that rise in happier climes,
The grot that heard his song of other times,
His cottage-home, his bark of slender sail,
His glassy lake, and broomwood blossom'd vale,
Rush on his thought; he sweeps before the wind,
Treads the lov'd shore he sigh'd to leave behind,
Meets at each step a friend's familiar face,
And flies at last to Helen's long embrace;
Wipes from her cheek the rapture-speaking tear,
And clasps, with many a sigh, his children dear!
While, long neglected, but at length caress'd,
His faithful dog salutes the smiling guest,
Points to the master's eyes (where'er they roam)
His wistful face, and whines a welcome home.

Friend of the brave! in peril's darkest hour,
Intrepid Virtue looks to thee for pow'r;
To thee the heart its trembling homage yields,
On stormy floods, and carnage-cover'd fields,
When front to front the banner'd hosts combine,
Halt ere they close, and form the dreadful line.
When all is still on Death's devoted soil,
The march-worn soldier mingles for the toil;
As rings his glittering tube, he lifts on high
The dauntless brow, and spirit-speaking eye,
Hails in his heart the triumph yet to come,
And hears thy stormy music in the drum!

And such thy strength-inspiring aid that bore
The hardy Byron to his native shore.—[1]
In horrid climes, where Chiloe's tempests sweep
Tumultuous murmurs o'er the troubled deep,
'Twas his to mourn misfortune's rudest shock,
Scourg'd by the winds, and cradled on the rock,
To wake each joyless morn, and search again
The famish'd haunts of solitary men,
Whose race, unyielding as their native storm,
Knows not a trace of Nature but the form;
Yet, at thy call, the hardy tar pursued,
Pale but intrepid, sad but unsubdued,
Pierc'd the deep woods, and, hailing from afar
The moon's pale planet and the northern star,
Paus'd at each dreary cry, unheard before,
Hyænas in the wild, and mermaids on the shore;
Till, led by thee o'er many a cliff sublime,
He found a warmer world, a milder clime,
A home to rest, a shelter to defend,
Peace and repose, a Briton and a friend![2]

Congenial Hope! thy passion-kindling pow'r,
How bright, how strong, in youth's untroubled hour!
On yon proud height, with genius hand in hand,
I see thee light, and wave thy golden wand.

"Go, Child of Heaven! (thy winged words proclaim,)
'Tis thine to search the boundless fields of fame!
Lo! Newton, Priest of Nature, shines afar,
Scans the wide world, and numbers every star!

Wilt thou, with him, mysterious rites apply,
And watch the shrine with wonder-beaming eye?
Yes, thou shalt mark, with magic art profound,
The speed of light, the circling march of sound;
With Franklin grasp the lightning's fiery wing,
Or yield the lyre of heav'n another string.[3]

"The Swedish sage admires, in yonder bow'rs,[4]
His winged insects, and his rosy flow'rs;
Calls from their woodland haunts the savage train
With sounding horn, and counts them on the plain—
So once, at Heav'n's command, the wand'rers came
To Eden's shade, and heard their various name.

"Far from the world, in yon sequester'd clime,
Slow pass the sons of Wisdom, more sublime;
Calm as the fields of heav'n, his sapient eye
The lov'd Athenian lifts to realms on high,
Admiring Plato on his spotless page,
Stamps the bright dictates of the Father sage:
'Shall Nature bound to Earth's diurnal span,
The fire of God, th' immortal soul of man?'

"Turn, Child of Heav'n, thy rapture-lighten'd eye
To Wisdom's walks, the sacred Nine are nigh:
Hark! from bright spires that gild the Delphian height,
From streams that wander in eternal light,
Rang'd on their hill, Harmonia's daughters swell
The mingling tones of horn, and harp, and shell;
Deep from his vaults, the Loxian murmurs flow,[5]
And Pythia's awful organ peals below.

"Belov'd of Heav'n! the smiling muse shall shed
Her moonlight halo on thy beauteous head;
Shall swell thy heart to rapture unconfin'd,
And breathe a holy madness o'er thy mind.

I see thee roam her guardian pow'r beneath,
And talk with spirits on the midnight heath;

Inquire of guilty wand'rers whence they came,
And ask each blood-stain'd form his earthly name;
Then weave in rapid verse the deeds they tell,
And read the trembling world the tales of hell.

"When Venus, thron'd in clouds of rosy hue,
Flings from her golden urn the vesper dew,
And bids fond man her glimmering noon employ,
Sacred to love and walks of tender joy;
A milder mood the goddess shall recall,
And soft as dew thy tones of music fall:
While Beauty's deeply pictur'd smiles impart
A pang more dear than pleasure to the heart—
Warm as thy sighs shall flow the Lesbian strain,
And plead in Beauty's ear, nor plead in vain.

"Or wilt thou Orphean hymns more sacred deem,
And steep thy song in Mercy's mellow stream;
To pensive drops the radiant eye beguile—
For Beauty's tears are lovelier than her smile;—
On Nature's throbbing anguish pour relief,
And teach impassion'd souls the Joy of Grief?

"Yes; to thy tongue shall seraph words be giv'n,
And pow'r on earth to plead the cause of Heav'n;
The proud, the cold untroubled heart of stone,
That never mus'd on sorrow but its own,
Unlocks a generous store at thy command,
Like Horeb's rocks beneath the prophet's hand.[6]
The living lumber of his kindred earth,
Charm'd into soul, receives a second birth;
Feels thy dread pow'r another heart afford,
Whose passion-touch'd harmonious strings accord

True as the circling spheres to Nature's plan;
And man, the brother, lives the friend of man!

"Bright as the pillar rose at Heav'n's command,
When Israel march'd along the desert land,

Blaz'd through the night on lonely wilds afar,
And told the path—a never-setting star:
So, heav'nly Genius, in thy course divine,
Hope is thy star, her light is ever thine."

Propitious Pow'r! when rankling cares annoy
The sacred home of Hymenean joy;
When doom'd to Poverty's sequester'd dell,
The wedded pair of love and virtue dwell,
Unpitied by the world, unknown to fame,
Their woes, their wishes, and their hearts the same—

Oh there, prophetic Hope! thy smile bestow,
And chase the pangs that worth should never know—
There, as the parent deals his scanty store
To friendless babes, and weeps to give no more;
Tell, that his manly race shall yet assuage
Their father's wrongs, and shield his later age.
What though for him no Hybla sweets distil,
Nor bloomy vines wave purple on the hill;
Tell, that when silent years have pass'd away,
That when his eye grows dim, his tresses gray,
These busy hands a lovelier cot shall build,
And deck with fairer flow'rs his little field,

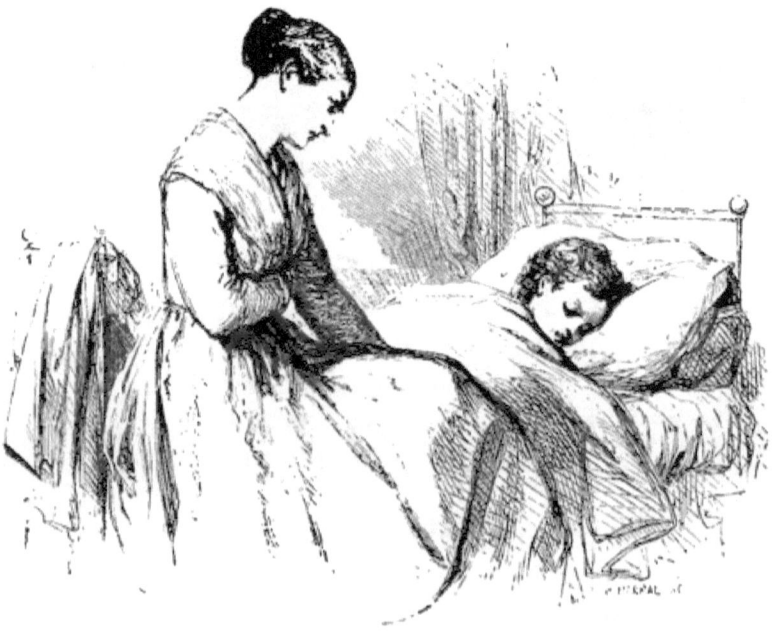

And call from Heav'n propitious dews to breathe
Arcadian beauty on the barren heath;

Tell, that while Love's spontaneous smile endears
The days of peace, the Sabbath of his years,
Health shall prolong to many a festive hour
The social pleasures of his humble bow'r.

Lo! at the couch where infant beauty sleeps,
Her silent watch the mournful mother keeps;
She, while the lovely babe unconscious lies,
Smiles on her slumb'ring child with pensive eyes,
And weaves a song of melancholy joy—
"Sleep, image of thy father, sleep, my boy:
No ling'ring hour of sorrow shall be thine;
No sigh that rends thy father's heart and mine;
Bright as his manly sire, the son shall be
In form and soul; but, ah! more blest than he!
Thy fame, thy worth, thy filial love, at last,
Shall soothe this aching heart for all the past—
With many a smile my solitude repay,
And chase the world's ungen'rous scorn away.

"And say, when summon'd from the world and thee,
I laid my head beneath the willow tree;
Wilt *thou*, sweet mourner! at my stone appear,
And soothe my parted spirit ling'ring near?
Oh, wilt thou come, at ev'ning hour, to shed
The tears of Memory o'er my narrow bed;
With aching temples on thy hand reclin'd,
Muse on the last farewell I leave behind,
Breathe a deep sigh to winds that murmur low,
And think on all my love, and all my woe?"

So speaks affection, ere the infant eye
Can look regard, or brighten in reply;

But when the cherub lip hath learnt to claim
A mother's ear by that endearing name;
Soon as the playful innocent can prove
A tear of pity, or a smile of love,
Or cons his murm'ring task beneath her care,
Or lisps with holy look his ev'ning prayer,

Or gazing, mutely pensive, sits to hear
The mournful ballad warbled in his ear;
How fondly looks admiring Hope the while,
At ev'ry artless tear, and ev'ry smile!
How glows the joyous parent to descry
A guileless bosom, true to sympathy!

Where is the troubled heart, consign'd to share
Tumultuous toils, or solitary care,
Unblest by visionary thoughts that stray
To count the joys of Fortune's better day!
Lo, nature, life, and liberty relume
The dim-ey'd tenant of the dungeon gloom,
A long-lost friend, or hapless child restor'd,
Smile at his blazing hearth and social board;
Warm from his heart the tears of rapture flow,
And virtue triumphs o'er remember'd woe.

Chide not his peace, proud Reason! nor destroy
The shadowy forms of uncreated joy,
That urge the lingering tide of life, and pour
Spontaneous slumber on his midnight hour.

Hark! the wild maniac sings, to chide the gale
That wafts so slow her lover's distant sail;
She, sad spectatress, on the wint'ry shore
Watch'd the rude surge his shroudless corse that bore,
Knew the pale form, and, shrieking in amaze,
Clasp'd her cold hands, and fix'd her maddening gaze:
Poor widow'd wretch! 'twas there she wept in vain,
Till memory fled her agonizing brain;—
But Mercy gave, to charm the sense of woe,
Ideal peace, that Truth could ne'er bestow;—
Warm on her heart the joys of Fancy beam,
And aimless Hope delights her darkest dream.

Oft when yon moon has climb'd the midnight sky,
And the lone sea-bird wakes its wildest cry,

Pil'd on the steep, her blazing faggots burn
To hail the bark that never can return;

And still she waits, but scarce forbears to weep
That constant love can linger on the deep.

And, mark the wretch whose wanderings never knew
The world's regard, that soothes, though half untrue
Whose erring heart the lash of sorrow bore,
But found not pity when it err'd no more.

Yon friendless man, at whose dejected eye
Th' unfeeling proud one looks—and passes by;

Condemn'd on Penury's barren path to roam,
Scorn'd by the world, and left without a home—
Ev'n he, at evening, should he chance to stray
Down by the hamlet's hawthorn-scented way,
Where, round the cot's romantic glade are seen
The blossom'd bean-field, and the sloping green,
Leans o'er its humble gate, and thinks the while—
" Oh that for me some home like this would smile,
Some hamlet shade, to yield my sickly form,
Health in the breeze, and shelter in the storm!
There should my hand no stinted boon assign
To wretched hearts with sorrows such as mine;"—
That generous wish can soothe unpitied care,
And Hope half mingles with the poor man's prayer.

Hope! when I mourn, with sympathising mind,
The wrongs of fate, the woes of human kind,
Thy blissful omens bid my spirit see
The boundless fields of rapture yet to be;
I watch the wheels of Nature's mazy plan,
And learn the future by the past of man.

Come, bright Improvement! on the car of Time,
And rule the spacious world from clime to clime;
Thy handmaid arts shall every wild explore,
Trace every wave, and culture every shore.
On Erie's banks, where tigers steal along,
And the dread Indian chants a dismal song;
Where human fiends on midnight errands walk,
And bathe in brains the murd'rous tomahawk;
There shall the flocks on thymy pasture stray,
And shepherds dance at Summer's opening day;

Each wandering genius of the lonely glen
Shall start to view the glittering haunts of men;

And silent watch, on woodland heights around,
The village curfew, as it tolls profound.

In Libyan groves, where damnèd rites are done
That bathe the rocks in blood, and veil the sun,
Truth shall arrest the murd'rous arm profane,
Wild Obi flies[7]—the veil is rent in twain.

Where barb'rous hordes on Scythian mountains roam,
Truth, Mercy, Freedom, yet shall find a home;
Where'er degraded Nature bleeds and pines,
From Guinea's coast to Sibir's dreary mines,[8]
Truth shall pervade th' unfathom'd darkness there,
And light the dreadful features of despair.—
Hark! the stern captive spurns his heavy load,
And asks the image back that Heaven bestow'd
Fierce in his eye the fire of valour burns,
And, as the slave departs, the man returns!

Oh! sacred Truth! thy triumph ceas'd a while,
And Hope, thy sister, ceas'd with thee to smile,
When leagued Oppression pour'd to Northern wars
Her whisker'd pandoors and her fierce hussars,
Wav'd her dread standard to the breeze of morn,
Peal'd her loud drum, and twang'd her trumpet horn
Tumultuous horror brooded o'er her van,
Presaging wrath to Poland—and to man![9]

Warsaw's last champion from her height survey'd,
Wide o'er the fields, a waste of ruin laid,—
"Oh! Heav'n!" he cried, "my bleeding country save!—
Is there no hand on high to shield the brave?—

Yet, though destruction sweep these lovely plains,
Rise, fellow-men! our country yet remains!
By that dread name, we wave the sword on high,
And swear for her to live!—with her to die!"

He said, and on the rampart heights array'd
His trusty warriors, few, but undismay'd;
Firm-pac'd and slow, a horrid front they form,
Still as the breeze, but dreadful as the storm;

Low murm'ring sounds along their banners fly,
Revenge, or death,—the watchword and reply;
Then peal'd the notes, omnipotent to charm,
And the loud tocsin toll'd their last alarm!—

In vain, alas! in vain, ye gallant few!
From rank to rank your volley'd thunder flew:—
Oh! bloodiest picture in the book of Time,
Sarmatia fell, unwept, without a crime;
Found not a gen'rous friend, a pitying foe,
Strength in her arms, nor mercy in her woe!
Dropp'd from her nerveless grasp the shatter'd spear,
Clos'd her bright eye, and curb'd her high career;—
Hope, for a season, bade the world farewell,
And Freedom shriek'd—as KOSCIUSKO fell!

The sun went down, nor ceas'd the carnage there,
Tumultuous murder shook the midnight air—
On Prague's proud arch the fires of ruin glow,
His blood-dyed waters murm'ring far below;—
The storm prevails, the rampart yields a way,
Bursts the wild cry of horror and dismay!—
Hark! as the smouldering piles with thunder fall,
A thousand shrieks for hopeless mercy call!
Earth shook—red meteors flash'd along the sky,
And conscious Nature shudder'd at the cry!

Oh! righteous Heav'n! ere Freedom found a grave,
Why slept the sword, omnipotent to save?
Where was thine arm, O Vengeance! where thy rod,
That smote the foes of Zion and of God;
That crush'd proud Ammon, when his iron car
Was yok'd in wrath, and thunder'd from afar?

Where was the storm that slumber'd till the host
Of blood-stain'd Pharaoh left their trembling coast,
Then bade the deep in wild commotion flow,
And heav'd an ocean on their march below?

Departed spirits of the mighty dead!
Ye that at Marathon and Leuctra bled!
Friends of the world! restore your swords to man,
Fight in his sacred cause, and lead the van!
Yet for Sarmatia's tears of blood atone,
And make her arm puissant as your own!—
Oh! once again to Freedom's cause return
The patriot TELL—the BRUCE OF BANNOCKBURN!

Yes! thy proud lords, unpitied land! shall see
That man hath yet a soul—and dare be free!
A little while, along thy sadd'ning plains,
The starless night of Desolation reigns;
Truth shall restore the light by Nature giv'n,
And, like Prometheus, bring the fire of Heav'n
Prone to the dust Oppression shall be hurl'd,
Her name, her nature, wither'd from the world!

Ye that the rising morn invidious mark,
And hate the light—because your deeds are dark;
Ye that expanding truth invidious view,
And think, or wish, the song of Hope untrue;
Perhaps your little hands presume to span
The march of Genius, and the pow'rs of man;
Perhaps ye watch, at Pride's unhallow'd shrine,
Her victims, newly slain, and thus divine:—
"Here shall thy triumph, Genius, cease, and here,
Truth, Science, Virtue, close your short career."

Tyrants! in vain ye trace the wizard ring;
In vain ye limit Mind's unwearied spring:
What! can ye lull the wingèd winds asleep,
Arrest the rolling world, or chain the deep?
No!—the wild wave contemns your sceptred hand;—
It roll'd not back when Canute gave command!

Man! can thy doom no brighter soul allow?
Still must thou live a blot on Nature's brow?
Shall War's polluted banner ne'er be furl'd?
Shall crimes and tyrants cease but with the world?
What! are thy triumphs, Sacred Truth, belied?
Why then hath Plato liv'd—or Sidney died?

Ye fond adorers of departed fame,
Who warm at Scipio's worth, or Tully's name!
Ye that, in fancied vision, can admire
The sword of Brutus, and the Theban lyre!
Rapt in historic ardour, who adore
Each classic haunt and well-remember'd shore,
Where Valour tun'd, amid her chosen throng,
The Thracian trumpet and the Spartan song;
Or, wand'ring thence, behold the later charms
Of England's glory, and Helvetia's arms!
See Roman fire in Hampden's bosom swell,
And fate and freedom in the shaft of Tell!
Say, ye fond zealots to the worth of yore,
Hath Valour left the world—to live no more?
No more shall Brutus bid a tyrant die,
And sternly smile with vengeance in his eye?
Hampden no more, when suff'ring Freedom calls,
Encounter Fate, and triumph as he falls?

Nor Tell disclose, through peril and alarm,
The might that slumbers in a peasant's arm?

Yes! in that gen'rous cause, for ever strong,
The patriot's virtue and the poet's song,
Still, as the tide of ages rolls away,
Shall charm the world, unconscious of decay.

Yes! there are hearts, prophetic Hope may trust,
That slumber yet in uncreated dust,
Ordain'd to fire th' adoring sons of earth
With every charm of wisdom and of worth;

Ordain'd to light, with intellectual day,
The mazy wheels of Nature as they play,
Or, warm with Fancy's energy, to glow,
And rival all but Shakspeare's name below.

And say, supernal Powers! who deeply scan
Heaven's dark decrees, unfathom'd yet by man,
When shall the world call down, to cleanse her shame,
That embryo spirit, yet without a name,—
That friend of Nature, whose avenging hands
Shall burst the Libyan's adamantine bands?
Who, sternly marking on his native soil,
The blood, the tears, the anguish, and the toil,
Shall bid each righteous heart exult, to see
Peace to the slave, and vengeance on the free!

Yet, yet, degraded men! th' expected day
That breaks your bitter cup, is far away;
Trade, wealth, and fashion, ask you still to bleed,
And holy men give Scripture for the deed;
Scourg'd and debas'd, no Briton stoops to save
A wretch, a coward; yes, because a slave!—

Eternal Nature! when thy giant hand
Had heav'd the floods, and fix'd the trembling land,
When life sprang startling at thy plastic call,
Endless her forms, and Man the lord of all!
Say, was that lordly form inspir'd by thee
To wear eternal chains, and bow the knee?
Was man ordain'd the slave of man to toil,
Yok'd with the brutes, and fetter'd to the soil;
Weigh'd in a tyrant's balance with his gold?
No!—Nature stamp'd us in a heavenly mould!

She bade no wretch his thankless labour urge,
Nor, trembling, take the pittance and the scourge!
No homeless Libyan, on the stormy deep,
To call upon his country's name, and weep!—

  Lo! once in triumph on his boundless plain,
The quiver'd chief of Congo lov'd to reign;
With fires proportion'd to his native sky,
Strength in his arm, and lightning in his eye;
Scour'd with wild feet his sun-illumin'd zone,
The spear, the lion, and the woods his own!
Or led the combat, bold without a plan,
An artless savage, but a fearless man!

  The plunderer came!—alas! no glory smiles
For Congo's chief on yonder Indian isles;
For ever fallen! no son of Nature now,
With freedom charter'd on his manly brow!
Faint, bleeding, bound, he weeps the night away,
And, when the sea-wind wafts the dewless day,
Starts, with a bursting heart, for ever more
To curse the sun that lights their guilty shore!

  The shrill horn blew;[10] at that alarum knell
His guardian angel took a last farewell!
That funeral dirge to darkness hath resign'd
The fiery grandeur of a generous mind!
Poor fetter'd man! I hear thee whispering low
Unhallow'd vows to Guilt, the child of Woe:
Friendless thy heart, and canst thou harbour there
A wish but death—a passion but despair?

  The widow'd Indian, when her lord expires,
Mounts the dread pile, and braves the funeral fires!

So falls the heart at Thraldom's bitter sigh!
So Virtue dies, the spouse of Liberty!

  But not to Libya's barren climes alone,
To Chili, or the wild Siberian zone,
Belong the wretched heart and haggard eye,
Degraded worth, and poor misfortune's sigh!—
Ye orient realms, where Ganges' waters run!
Prolific fields! dominions of the sun!
How long your tribes have trembled and obey'd!
How long was Timour's iron sceptre sway'd,[11]
Whose marshall'd hosts, the lions of the plain,
From Scythia's northern mountains to the main,
Raged o'er your plunder'd shrines and altars bare,
With blazing torch and gory scimitar,—
Stunn'd with the cries of death each gentle gale,
And bath'd in blood the verdure of the vale!
Yet could no pangs the immortal spirit tame,
When Brama's children perish'd for his name;
The martyr smil'd beneath avenging power,
And brav'd the tyrant in his torturing hour!

  When Europe sought your subject realms to gain,
And stretch'd her giant sceptre o'er the main,
Taught her proud barks their winding way to shape,
And brav'd the stormy spirit of the Cape;[12]
Children of Brama! then was mercy nigh
To wash the stain of blood's eternal dye?
Did Peace descend, to triumph and to save,
When free-born Britons cross'd the Indian wave?
Ah, no!—to more than Rome's ambition true,
The Nurse of Freedom gave it not to you!

She the bold route of Europe's guilt began,
And, in the march of nations, led the van!

Rich in the gems of India's gaudy zone,
And plunder pil'd from kingdoms not their own,
Degenerate Trade! thy minions could despise
The heart-born anguish of a thousand cries

Could lock, with impious hands, their teeming store,
While famish'd nations died along the shore;[13]
Could mock the groans of fellow-men, and bear
The curse of kingdoms peopled with despair;
Could stamp disgrace on man's polluted name,
And barter, with their gold, eternal shame!

But hark! as bow'd to earth the Bramin kneels,
From heavenly climes propitious thunder peals!
Of India's fate her guardian spirits tell,
Prophetic murmurs breathing on the shell,
And solemn sounds, that awe the list'ning mind,
Roll on the azure paths of ev'ry wind.

"Foes of mankind! (her guardian spirits say,)
Revolving ages bring the bitter day,
When Heaven's unerring arm shall fall on you,
And blood for blood these Indian plains bedew;
Nine times have Brama's wheels of lightning hurl'd
His awful presence o'er the alarmed world;
Nine times hath Guilt, through all his giant frame,
Convulsive trembled as the Mighty came:
Nine times hath suffering Mercy spar'd in vain[14]—
But Heaven shall burst her starry gates again!
He comes! dread Brama shakes the sunless sky
With murmuring wrath, and thunders from on high!
Heaven's fiery horse, beneath his warrior form,
Paws the light clouds, and gallops on the storm!
Wide waves his flickering sword; his bright arms glow
Like summer suns, and light the world below!
Earth, and her trembling isles in Ocean's bed,
Are shook, and Nature rocks beneath his tread!

"To pour redress on India's injured realm,
The oppressor to dethrone, the proud to whelm;
To chase destruction from her plunder'd shore
With arts and arms that triumph'd once before,
The tenth Avatar comes! at Heaven's command
Shall Seriswattee[15] wave her hallow'd wand!
And Camdeo bright, and Ganesa sublime,
Shall bless with joy their own propitious clime!—
Come, Heav'nly Powers! primeval peace restore!
Love!—Mercy!—Wisdom!—rule for evermore!"

ANALYSIS OF PART II.

APOSTROPHE to the power of Love.—Its intimate connexion with generous and social Sensibility.—Allusion to that beautiful passage in the beginning of the Book of Genesis, which represents the happiness of Paradise itself incomplete, till Love was superadded to its other blessings.—The dreams of future felicity which a lively imagination is apt to cherish, when Hope is animated by refined attachment.—This disposition to combine, in one imaginary scene of residence, all that is pleasing in our estimate of happiness, compared to the skill of the great artist, who personified perfect beauty, in the picture of Venus, by an assemblage of the most beautiful features he could find.—A summer and winter evening described, as they may be supposed to arise in the mind of one who wishes, with enthusiasm, for the union of friendship and retirement.

Hope and Imagination inseparable agents.—Even in those contemplative moments when our imagination wanders beyond the boundaries of this world, our minds are not unattended with an impression, that we shall some day have a wider and more distinct prospect of the universe, instead of the partial glimpse we now enjoy.

The last and most sublime influence of Hope is the concluding topic of the Poem.—The predominance of a belief in a future state over the terrors attendant on dissolution.—The baneful influence of that sceptical philosophy which bars us from such comforts.—Allusion to the fate of a suicide.—Episode of Conrad and Ellenore.—Conclusion.

PART II.

In joyous youth, what soul hath never known
Thought, feeling, taste, harmonious to its own?
Who hath not paus'd, while Beauty's pensive eye
Ask'd from his heart the homage of a sigh?
Who hath not own'd, with rapture-smitten frame,
The power of grace, the magic of a name?

F

There be, perhaps, who barren hearts avow,
Cold as the rocks on Torneo's hoary brow;
There be, whose loveless wisdom never fail'd,
In self-adoring pride securely mail'd :—
But, triumph not, ye peace-enamour'd few!
Fire, Nature, Genius, never dwelt with you!
For you no fancy consecrates the scene
Where rapture utter'd vows, and wept between:
'Tis yours, unmov'd, to sever and to meet;
No pledge is sacred, and no home is sweet!

Who that would ask a heart to dulness wed,
The waveless calm, the slumber of the dead?
No; the wild bliss of Nature needs alloy,
And fear and sorrow fan the fire of joy!
And say, without our hopes, without our fears,
Without the home that plighted love endears,
Without the smile from partial beauty won,
Oh! what were man?—a world without a sun!

Till Hymen brought his love-delighted hour,
There dwelt no joy in Eden's rosy bow'r!
In vain the viewless seraph ling'ring there,
At starry midnight, charm'd the silent air;
In vain, the wild-bird caroll'd on the steep,
To hail the sun, slow-wheeling from the deep;
In vain, to soothe the solitary shade,
Aërial notes in mingling measure play'd;
The summer wind that shook the spangled tree,
The whispering wave, the murmur of the bee;—
Still slowly pass'd the melancholy day,
And still the stranger wist not where to stray.

The world was sad!—the garden was a wild!
And man, the hermit, sigh'd—till Woman smil'd!

True, the sad power to gen'rous hearts may bring
Delirious anguish on his fiery wing!
Barr'd from delight by Fate's untimely hand,
By wealthless lot, or pitiless command;
Or doom'd to gaze on beauties that adorn
The smile of triumph, or the frown of scorn;
While Memory watches o'er the sad review
Of joys that faded like the morning dew;
Peace may depart—and life and nature seem
A barren path—a wildness, and a dream!

But can the noble mind for ever brood,
The willing victim of a weary mood,

On heartless cares that squander life away,
And cloud young Genius bright'ning into day!—
Shame to the coward thought that e'er betray'd
The noon of manhood to a myrtle shade!—
If Hope's creative spirit cannot raise
One trophy sacred to thy future days,
Scorn the dull crowd that haunt the gloomy shrine,
Of hopeless love to murmur and repine!
But, should a sigh of milder mood express
Thy heart-warm wishes, true to happiness,
Should Heaven's fair harbinger delight to pour
Her blissful visions on thy pensive hour,
No tear to blot thy memory's pictur'd page,
No fears but such as fancy can assuage;
Through thy wild heart some hapless hour may miss
The peaceful tenor of unvaried bliss,
(For love pursues an ever-devious race,
True to the winding lineaments of grace;)
Yet still may Hope her talisman employ
To snatch from Heaven anticipated joy,
And all her kindred energies impart
That burn the brightest in the purest heart!

When first the Rhodian's mimic art array'd
The queen of Beauty in her Cyprian shade,
The happy master mingled on his piece
Each look that charm'd him in the fair of Greece.
To faultless Nature true, he stole a grace
From every finer form and sweeter face;
And, as he sojourn'd on the Ægean isles,
Woo'd all their love, and treasur'd all their smiles!
Then glow'd the tints, pure, precious, and refin'd,
And mortal charms seem'd heav'nly when combin'd!

Love on the picture smil'd! Expression pour'd
Her mingling spirit there—and Greece ador'd!

So thy fair hand, enamour'd Fancy! gleans
The treasur'd pictures of a thousand scenes;
Thy pencil traces on the Lover's thought
Some cottage-home, from towns and toil remote,
Where Love and Lore may claim alternate hours,
With Peace embosom'd in Idalian bow'rs!
Remote from busy Life's bewilder'd way,
O'er all his heart shall Taste and Beauty sway;
Free on the sunny slope, or winding shore,
With hermit steps to wander and adore!

There shall he love, when genial morn appears,
Like pensive Beauty smiling in her tears,

To watch the bright'ning roses of the sky,
And muse on Nature with a poet's eye!—
And when the sun's last splendour lights the deep,
The woods and waves and murm'ring winds asleep;
When fairy harps th' Hesperian planet hail,
And the lone cuckoo sighs along the vale,
His path shall be where streamy mountains swell
Their shadowy grandeur o'er the narrow dell,
Where mouldering piles and forests intervene,
Mingling with darker tints the living green;
No circling hills his ravish'd eye to bound,
Heaven, Earth, and Ocean blazing all around.

The moon is up—the watch-tow'r dimly burns,—
And down the vale his sober step returns;
But pauses oft, as winding rocks convey
The still sweet fall of Music far away;
And oft he lingers from his home awhile
To watch the dying notes!—and start, and smile!

Let Winter come! let polar spirits sweep
The dark'ning world, and tempest-troubled deep!
Though boundless snows the wither'd heath deform,
And the dim sun scarce wanders through the storm,
Yet shall the smile of social love repay,
With mental light, the melancholy day!
And, when its short and sullen noon is o'er,
The ice-chain'd waters slumb'ring on the shore,
How bright the fagots in his little hall
Blaze on the hearth, and warm the pictur'd wall!

How blest he names, in Love's familiar tone,
The kind fair friend, by Nature mark'd his own;

And, in the waveless mirror of his mind,
Views the fleet years of pleasure left behind,
Since when her empire o'er his heart began!
Since first he call'd her his before the holy man!
  Trim the gay taper in his rustic dome,
And light the wint'ry paradise of home;
And let the half-uncurtain'd window hail
Some way-worn man benighted in the vale!

Now, while the moaning night-wind rages high,
As sweep the shot-stars down the troubled sky,
While fiery hosts in heaven's wide circle play,
And bathe in lurid light the milky way,

Safe from the storm, the meteor, and the shower,
Some pleasing page shall charm the solemn hour—
With pathos shall command, with wit beguile,
A gen'rous tear of anguish, or a smile—
Thy woes, Arion! and thy simple tale,[2]
O'er all the heart shall triumph and prevail!
Charm'd as they read the verse too sadly true,
How gallant Albert, and his weary crew,
Heav'd all their guns, their foundering bark to save,
And toil'd—and shriek'd—and perish'd on the wave!

Yes, at the dead of night, by Lonna's steep,
The seaman's cry was heard along the deep;
There on his funeral waters, dark and wild,
The dying father blest his darling child!
"Oh! Mercy, shield her innocence," he cried,
Spent on the pray'r his bursting heart, and died!

Or they will learn how gen'rous worth sublimes
The robber Moor,[3] and pleads for all his crimes!
How poor Amelia kiss'd, with many a tear,
His hand blood-stain'd, but ever, ever dear!
Hung on the tortur'd bosom of her lord,
And wept, and pray'd perdition from his sword!
Nor sought in vain! at that heart-piercing cry
The strings of nature crack'd with agony!
He, with delirious laugh, the dagger hurl'd,
And burst the ties that bound him to the world!

Turn from his dying words, that smite with steel
The shuddering thoughts, or wind them on the wheel—
Turn to the gentler melodies that suit
Thalia's harp, or Pan's Arcadian lute;

Or, down the stream of Truth's historic page,
From clime to clime descend, from age to age!

Yet there, perhaps, may darker scenes obtrude
Than Fancy fashions in her wildest mood;

There shall he pause, with horrent brow, to rate
What millions died—that Cæsar might be great![4]
Or learn the fate that bleeding thousands bore,[5]
March'd by their Charles to Dnieper's swampy shore;
Faint in his wounds, and shivering in the blast,
The Swedish soldier sunk—and groan'd his last!
File after file the stormy showers benumb,
Freeze every standard-sheet, and hush the drum!
Horseman and horse confess'd the bitter pang,
And arms and warriors fell with hollow clang!
Yet, ere he sunk in Nature's last repose,
Ere life's warm torrent to the fountain froze,
The dying man to Sweden turn'd his eye,
Thought of his home, and clos'd it with a sigh!
Imperial Pride look'd sullen on his plight,
And Charles beheld—nor shudder'd at the sight!

    Above, below, in Ocean, Earth, and Sky,
Thy fairy worlds, Imagination, lie,
And Hope attends, companion of the way,
Thy dream by night, thy visions of the day!
In yonder pensile orb, and every sphere
That gems the starry girdle of the year;
In those unmeasur'd worlds, she bids thee tell,
Pure from their God, created millions dwell,
Whose names and natures, unreveal'd below,
We yet shall learn, and wonder as we know;
For, as Iona's Saint, a giant form,[6]
Thron'd on her tow'rs, conversing with the storm,
(When o'er each Runic altar, weed-entwin'd,
The vesper clock tolls mournful to the wind,)
Counts every wave-worn isle, and mountain hoar,
From Kilda to the green Ierne's shore;

So, when thy pure and renovated mind
This perishable dust hath left behind,
Thy seraph eye shall count the starry train,
Like distant isles embosom'd in the main;

Rapt to the shrine where motion first began,
And light and life in mingling torrent ran;
From whence each bright rotundity was hurl'd,
The throne of God,—the centre of the world!

Oh! vainly wise, the moral Muse hath sung
That suasive Hope hath but a Syren tongue!
True; she may sport with life's untutor'd day,
Nor heed the solace of its last decay,
The guileless heart her happy mansion spurn,
And part like Ajut—never to return![7]

But yet, methinks, when Wisdom shall assuage
The griefs and passions of our greener age,
Though dull the close of life, and far away
Each flow'r that hail'd the dawning of the day;

Yet o'er her lovely hopes that once were dear,
The time-taught spirit, pensive, not severe,
With milder griefs her aged eye shall fill,
And weep their falsehood, though she loves them still!

Thus, with forgiving tears, and reconcil'd,
The king of Judah mourn'd his rebel child!
Musing on days, when yet the guiltless boy
Smil'd on his sire, and fill'd his heart with joy!
"My Absalom!" the voice of Nature cried;
"Oh that for thee thy father could have died!
For bloody was the deed, and rashly done,
That slew my Absalom!—my son!—my son!"

Unfading Hope! when life's last embers burn,
When soul to soul, and dust to dust return!
Heav'n to thy charge resigns the awful hour!
Oh! then, thy kingdom comes! Immortal Pow'r!
What though each spark of earth-born rapture fly
The quivering lip, pale cheek, and closing eye!
Bright to the soul thy seraph hands convey
The morning dream of life's eternal day—
Then, then, the triumph and the trance begin,
And all the Phœnix spirit burns within!

Oh! deep-enchanting prelude to repose,
The dawn of bliss, the twilight of our woes!
Yet half I hear the parting spirit sigh,
"It is a dread and awful thing to die!"
Mysterious worlds, untravell'd by the sun!
Where Time's far-wand'ring tide has never run,
From your unfathom'd shades, and viewless spheres,
A warning comes, unheard by other ears.

'Tis Heaven's commanding trumpet, long and loud,
Like Sinai's thunder, pealing from the cloud!
While Nature hears, with terror-mingled trust,
The shock that hurls her fabric to the dust;
And, like the trembling Hebrew, when he trod
The roaring waves, and call'd upon his God,
With mortal terrors clouds immortal bliss,
And shrieks, and hovers o'er the dark abyss!

  Daughter of Faith, awake, arise, illume
The dread unknown, the chaos of the tomb!
Melt, and dispel, ye spectre-doubts, that roll
Cimmerian darkness o'er the parting soul!
Fly, like the moon-ey'd herald of dismay,
Chas'd on his night-steed by the star of day!
The strife is o'er—the pangs of Nature close,
And life's last rapture triumphs o'er her woes.
Hark! as the spirit eyes, with eagle gaze,
The noon of heav'n undazzled by the blaze,
On heav'nly winds that waft her to the sky,
Float the sweet tones of star-born melody;
Wild as that hallow'd anthem sent to hail
Bethlehem's shepherds in the lonely vale,
When Jordan hush'd his waves, and midnight still
Watch'd on the holy tow'rs of Zion hill!

  Soul of the just! companion of the dead!
Where is thy home, and whither art thou fled?
Back to its heav'nly source thy being goes,
Swift as the comet wheels to whence he rose;
Doom'd on his airy path a while to burn,
And doom'd, like thee, to travel, and return.—

Hark! from the world's exploding centre driv'n,
With sounds that shook the firmament of heav'n,

Careers the fiery giant, fast and far,
On bick'ring wheels and adamantine car;
From planet whirl'd to planet more remote,
He visits realms beyond the reach of thought;

But, wheeling homeward, when his course is run,
Curbs the red yoke, and mingles with the sun!
So hath the traveller of earth unfurl'd
Her trembling wings, emerging from the world;
And o'er the path by mortal never trod,
Sprung to her source, the bosom of her God!

  Oh! lives there, Heav'n! beneath thy dread expanse,
One hopeless, dark idolater of Chance,
Content to feed, with pleasures unrefin'd,
The lukewarm passions of a lowly mind;
Who, mould'ring earthward, 'reft of every trust,
In joyless union wedded to the dust,
Could all his parting energy dismiss,
And call this barren world sufficient bliss?—
There live, alas! of Heav'n-directed mien,
Of cultur'd soul, and sapient eye serene,
Who hail thee, Man! the pilgrim of a day,
Spouse of the worm, and brother of the clay,
Frail as the leaf in Autumn's yellow bower,
Dust in the wind, or dew upon the flower,
A friendless slave, a child without a sire,
Whose mortal life, and momentary fire,
Light to the grave his chance-created form,
As ocean-wrecks illuminate the storm;
And, when the gun's tremendous flash is o'er,
To Night and Silence sink for evermore!—

  Are these the pompous tidings ye proclaim,
Lights of the world, and demi-gods of Fame?
Is this your triumph—this your proud applause,
Children of Truth, and champions of her cause?

For this hath Science search'd, on weary wing,
By shore and sea—each mute and living thing!
Launch'd with Iberia's pilot from the steep,
To worlds unknown, and isles beyond the deep,
Or round the cope her living chariot driv'n,
And wheel'd in triumph through the signs of heav'n?
Oh! star-ey'd Science, hast thou wander'd there,
To waft us home the message of despair?
Then bind the palm, thy sage's brow to suit,
Of blasted leaf and death distilling fruit!
Ah me! the laurell'd wreath that Murder rears,
Blood-nurs'd, and water'd by the widow's tears,
Seems not so foul, so tainted, and so dread,
As waves the night-shade round the sceptic head.
What is the bigot's torch, the tyrant's chain?
I smile on death, if heav'nward Hope remain!
But, if the warring winds of Nature's strife
Be all the faithless charter of my life,
If Chance awak'd, inexorable power!
This frail and fev'rish being of an hour,
Doom'd o'er the world's precarious scene to sweep,
Swift as the tempest travels on the deep,
To know Delight but by her parting smile,
And toil, and wish, and weep, a little while;
Then melt, ye elements, that form'd in vain
This troubled pulse, and visionary brain
Fade, ye wild flowers, memorials of my doom,
And sink, ye stars, that light me to the tomb!
Truth, ever lovely,—since the world began,
The foe of tyrants, and the friend of man,—
How can thy words from balmy slumber start
Reposing Virtue, pillow'd on the heart!

Yet, if thy voice the note of thunder roll'd,
And that were true which Nature never told;

Let Wisdom smile not on her conquer'd field;
No rapture dawns, no treasure is reveal'd!
Oh! let her read, nor loudly, nor elate,
The doom that bars us from a better fate;
But, sad as angels for the good man's sin,
Weep to record, and blush to give it in!

And well may Doubt, the mother of Dismay,
Pause at her martyr's tomb, and read the lay.
Down by the wilds of yon deserted vale,
It darkly hints a melancholy tale!
There, as the homeless madman sits alone
In hollow winds he hears a spirit moan!

And there, they say, a wizard orgie crowds,
When the moon lights her watch-tower in the clouds.
Poor lost Alonzo! Fate's neglected child!
Mild be the doom of Heav'n—as thou wert mild!
For oh! thy heart in holy mould was cast,
And all thy deeds were blameless, but the last.
Poor lost Alonzo! still I seem to hear
The clod that struck thy hollow-sounding bier!
When Friendship paid, in speechless sorrow drown'd,
Thy midnight rites, but not on hallow'd ground!

Cease, every joy, to glimmer on my mind,
But leave—oh! leave the light of Hope behind!
What though my winged hours of bliss have been,
Like angel-visits, few and far between,
Her musing mood shall every pang appease,
And charm—when pleasures lose the pow'r to please!

Yes; let each rapture, dear to Nature, flee;
Close not the light of Fortune's stormy sea—
Mirth, Music, Friendship, Love's propitious smile,
Chase every care, and charm a little while,
Ecstatic throbs the flutt'ring heart employ,
And all her strings are harmoniz'd to Joy!—
But why so short is Love's delighted hour?
Why fades the dew on Beauty's sweetest flow'r?
Why can no hymned charm of Music heal
The sleepless woes impassion'd spirits feel?
Can Fancy's fairy hands no veil create,
To hide the sad realities of fate?—

No! not the quaint remark, the sapient rule,
Nor all the pride of Wisdom's worldly school,

Have pow'r to soothe, unaided and alone,
The heart that vibrates to a feeling tone!
When stepdame Nature every bliss recalls,
Fleet as the meteor o'er the desert falls;
When, 'reft of all, yon widow'd sire appears
A lonely hermit in the vale of years;
Say, can the world one joyous thought bestow
To Friendship, weeping at the couch of Woe?
No! but a brighter soothes the last adieu,—
Souls of impassion'd mould, she speaks to you!
Weep not, she says, at Nature's transient pain,
Congenial spirits part to meet again!

What plaintive sobs thy filial spirit drew,
What sorrow chok'd thy long and last adieu,
Daughter of Conrad! when he heard his knell,
And bade his country and his child farewell!
Doom'd the long isles of Sydney Cove to see,
The martyr of his crimes, but true to thee.
Thrice the sad father tore thee from his heart,
And thrice return'd, to bless thee, and to part;
Thrice from his trembling lips he murmur'd low
The plaint that own'd unutterable woe;
Till Faith, prevailing o'er his sullen doom,
As bursts the morn on night's unfathom'd gloom,
Lur'd his dim eye to deathless hopes sublime,
Beyond the realms of Nature and of Time!

"And weep not thus," he cried, "young Ellenore!
My bosom bleeds, but soon shall bleed no more
Short shall this half-extinguish'd spirit burn,
And soon these limbs to kindred dust return!

But not, my child, with life's precarious fire,
Th' immortal ties of Nature shall expire;

These shall resist the triumph of decay,
When time is o'er, and worlds have pass'd away!
Cold in the dust this perish'd heart may lie,
But that which warm'd it once shall never die!
That spark unburied in its mortal frame,
With living light, eternal, and the same,
Shall beam on Joy's interminable years,
Unveil'd by darkness—unassuag'd by tears!

"Yet, on the barren shore and stormy deep,
One tedious watch is Conrad doom'd to weep;
But when I gain the home without a friend,
And press th' uneasy couch where none attend,
This last embrace, still cherish'd in my heart,
Shall calm the struggling spirit ere it part!
Thy darling form shall seem to hover nigh,
And hush the groan of life's last agony!

"Farewell! when strangers lift thy father's bier,
And place my nameless stone without a tear;
When each returning pledge hath told my child
That Conrad's tomb is on the desert pil'd;
And when the dream of troubled fancy sees
Its lonely rank-grass waving in the breeze;
Who then will soothe thy grief, when mine is o'er?
Who will protect thee, helpless Ellenore?
Shall secret scenes thy filial sorrows hide,
Scorn'd by the world, to factious guilt allied?
Ah! no; methinks the gen'rous and the good
Will woo thee from the shades of solitude!
O'er friendless grief Compassion shall awake,
And smile on innocence for Mercy's sake!"

Inspiring thought of rapture yet to be,
The tears of love were hopeless, but for thee!
If in that frame no deathless spirit dwell,
If that faint murmur be the last farewell,
If fate unite the faithful but to part,
Why is their memory sacred to the heart?
Why does the brother of my childhood seem
Restor'd a while in every pleasing dream?

Why do I joy the lonely spot to view,
By artless friendship blest when life was new?

 Eternal Hope! when yonder spheres sublime,
Peal'd their first notes to sound the march of Time,
Thy joyous youth began—but not to fade—
When all the sister planets have decay'd;
When rapt in fire the realms of ether glow,
And Heaven's last thunder shakes the world below
Thou, undismay'd, shalt o'er the ruin smile,
And light thy torch at Nature's funeral pile!

NOTES TO PART I.

(1.) *And such thy strength-inspiring aid that bore
The hardy Byron to his native shore.*

THE following picture of his own distress, given by Byron in his simple and interesting narrative, justifies the description in p. 6. After relating the barbarity of the Indian cacique to his child, he proceeds thus:—"A day or two after we put to sea again, and crossed the great bay I mentioned we had been at the bottom of, when we first hauled away to the westward. The land here was very low and sandy, and something like the mouth of a river which discharges itself into the sea, and which had been taken no notice of by us before, as it was so shallow that the Indians were obliged to take everything out of their canoes, and carry it over land. We rowed up the river four or five leagues, and then took into a branch of it that ran first to the eastward, and then to the northward: here it became much narrower, and the stream excessively rapid, so that we gained but little way, though we wrought very hard. At night we landed upon its banks, and had a most uncomfortable lodging, it being a perfect swamp; and we had nothing to cover us, though it rained excessively. The Indians were little better off than we, as there was no wood here to make their wigwams; so that all they could do was to prop up the bark which they carry in the bottom of their canoes, and shelter themselves as well as they could to the leeward of it. Knowing the difficulties they had to encounter here, they had provided themselves with some seal; but we had not a morsel to eat, after the heavy fatigues of the day, excepting a sort of root we saw the Indians make use of, which was very disagreeable to the taste. We laboured all next day against the stream, and fared as we had done the day before. The next day brought us to the carrying place. Here was plenty of wood, but nothing to be got for sustenance. We passed this night, as we had frequently done, under a tree; but what we suffered at this time is not easily to be expressed. I had been three days at the oar, without any kind of nourishment except the wretched root above mentioned. I had no shirt, for it had rotted off by bits. All my clothes consisted of a short grieko (something like a bearskin), a piece of red cloth which had once been a waistcoat, and a ragged pair of trowsers, without shoes or stockings."

(2.) *A Briton and a friend.*

Don Patricio Gedd, a Scotch physician in one of the Spanish settlements, hospitably relieved Byron and his wretched associates, of which the commodore speaks in the warmest terms of gratitude.

(3.) *Or yield the lyre of Heaven another string.*

The seven strings of Apollo's harp were the symbolical representation of the seven planets. Herschel, by discovering an eighth, might be said to add another string to the instrument.

(4.) *The Swedish sage.*

Linnæus.

(5.) *Deep from his vaults, the Loxian murmurs flow.*

Loxias is a name frequently given to Apollo by Greek writers: it is met with more than once in the Choephoræ of Æschylus.

(6.) *Unlocks a generous store at thy command,*
Like Horeb's rocks beneath the prophet's hand.

See Exodus, chap. xvii. 3, 5, 6.

(7.) *Wild Obi flies.*

Among the negroes of the West Indies, Obi, or Obiah, is the name of a magical power, which is believed by them to affect the object of its malignity with dismal calamities. Such a belief must undoubtedly have been deduced from the superstitious mythology of their kinsmen on the coast of Africa. I have, therefore, personified Obi as the evil spirit of the African, although the history of the African tribes mentions the evil spirit of their religious creed by a different appellation.

(8.) *Sibir's dreary mines.*

Mr. Bell of Antermony, in his Travels through Siberia, informs us that the name of the country is universally pronounced Sibir by the Russians.

(9.) *Presaging wrath to Poland—and to man.*

The history of the partition of Poland, of the massacre in the suburbs of Warsaw, and on the bridge of Prague, the triumphant entry of Suwarrow into the Polish capital, and the insult offered to human nature, by the blasphemous thanks offered up to Heaven, for victories obtained over men fighting in the sacred cause of liberty, by murderers and oppressors, are events generally known.

(10.) *The shrill horn blew.*

The negroes in the West Indies are summoned to their morning work by a shell or horn.

(11.) *How long was Timour's iron sceptre sway'd?*

To elucidate this passage, I shall subjoin a quotation from the Preface to Letters from a Hindoo Rajah, a work of elegance and celebrity.

"The impostor of Mecca had established, as one of the principles of his doctrine, the merit of extending it, either by persuasion or the sword, to all parts of the earth. How steadily this injunction was adhered to by his followers, and with what success it was pursued, is well known to all who are in the least conversant in history.

"The same overwhelming torrent which had inundated the greater part of Africa, burst its way into the very heart of Europe, and covered many kingdoms of Asia with unbounded desolation, directed its baneful course to the flourishing provinces of Hindostan. Here these fierce and hardy adventurers, whose only improvement had been in the science of destruction, who added the fury of fanaticism to the ravages of war, found the great end of their conquest opposed by objects which neither the ardour of their persevering zeal, nor savage barbarity, could surmount. Multitudes were sacrificed by the cruel hand of religious persecution, and whole countries were deluged in blood, in the vain hope that, by the destruction of a part, the remainder might be persuaded, or terrified into the profession of Mahomedism; but all these sanguinary efforts were ineffectual; and at length, being fully convinced that, though they might extirpate, they could never hope to convert, any number of the Hindoos, they relinquished the impracticable idea with which they had entered upon their career of conquest, and contented themselves with the acquirement of the civil dominion and almost universal empire of Hindostan."
—*Letters from a Hindoo Rajah,* by ELIZA HAMILTON.

(12.) *And braved the stormy spirit of the Cape.*

See the description of the Cape of Good Hope, translated from Camoens, by Mickle.

(13.) *While famish'd nations died along the shore.*

The following account of British conduct, and its consequences, in Bengal, will afford a sufficient idea of the fact alluded to in this passage. After describing the monopoly of salt, betel nut, and tobacco, the historian proceeds thus: "Money in this current came but by drops; it could not quench the thirst of those who waited in India to receive it. An expedient, such as it was, remained to quicken its pace. The natives could live with little salt, but could not want food. Some of the agents saw themselves well situated for collecting the rice into stores;—they did so. They knew the Gentoos would rather die than violate the principles of their religion by eating flesh. The alternative would therefore be between giving what they had, or dying. The inhabitants sunk;—they that cultivated the land, and saw the harvest at the disposal of others, planted in doubt—scarcity ensued. Then the monopoly was easier managed—sickness ensued. In some districts the languid living left the bodies of their numerous dead unburied."—*Short History of the English Transactions in the East Indies*, p. 145.

(14.) *Nine times have Brama's wheels of lightning hurl'd*
His awful presence o'er the alarmed world!

Among the sublime fictions of the Hindoo mythology, it is one article of belief, that the deity Brama has descended nine times upon the world in various forms, and that he is yet to appear a tenth time, in the figure of a warrior upon a white horse, to cut off all incorrigible offenders. Avatar is the word used to express his descent.

(15.) *And Camdeo bright, and Ganesa sublime.*

Camdeo is the God of Love in the mythology of the Hindoos. Ganesa and Seriswattee correspond to the Pagan deities, Janus and Minerva.

NOTES TO PART II.

(1.) *The noon of manhood to a myrtle shade!*

Sacred to Venus is the myrtle shade.—DRYDEN.

(2.) *Thy woes, Arion!*

Falconer, in his poem "The Shipwreck," speaks of himself by the name of Arion.

See Falconer's "Shipwreck," Canto III.

(3.) *The robber Moor.*

See Schiller's Tragedy of "The Robbers," Scene v.

(4.) *What millions died that Cæsar might be great!*

The carnage occasioned by the wars of Julius Cæsar has been usually estimated at two millions of men.

(5.) *Or learn the fate that bleeding thousands bore,*
March'd by their Charles to Dnieper's swampy shore.

In this extremity (says the biographer of Charles XII. of Sweden, speaking of his military exploits before the battle of Pultowa), the memorable winter of 1709, which was still more remarkable in that part of Europe than in France, destroyed numbers of his troops; for Charles resolved to brave the seasons as he had done his enemies, and ventured to make long marches during this mortal cold. It was in one of these marches that two thousand men fell down dead with cold before his eyes.

(6.) *For, as Iona's Saint.*

The natives of the island of St. Iona have an opinion, that on certain evenings every year the tutelary saint, Columba, is seen on the top of the church spires counting the surrounding islands, to see that they have not been sunk by the power of witchcraft.

(7.) *And part, like Ajut—never to return!*

See the history of Ajut and Anningait, in "The Rambler."

www.ingramcontent.com/pod-product-compliance
Lightning Source LLC
Chambersburg PA
CBHW020146170426
43199CB00010B/911